Home Baked

HOME BAKED

A little book of bread recipes

by

GEORGE AND
CECILIA SCURFIELD

with decorations by

NORA KAY

FABER AND FABER
24 Russell Square
London

*First published in mcmlvi
by Faber and Faber Limited
24 Russell Square London WC1
Second impression June mcmlvi
Third impression March mcmlix
Fourth impression December mcmlxv
Printed in Great Britain by
Latimer Trend & Co Ltd Plymouth*

To

ALICE ROUGHTON

who first taught us how

to make bread

Contents

Introduction

A few years ago we got fed up with shop bread. Even when quite fresh, it was unappetising; it was often poor in texture; sometimes it fell to bits on the board when we tried to slice it. And very often it wouldn't keep at all. As for wholemeal bread, this was practically unobtainable; the brown loaves we were offered seemed liked very distant cousins, several times removed.

We decided to bake our own bread. We had done this before occasionally but now we would go in for it more seriously. We were lucky enough to be living near a mill which still proudly produced a delightfully nutty, stone-ground, wholemeal flour. Their white flour, too, really tasted of wheat and was not just a fine, white

Introduction

powder like the tasteless stuff you bny in packets from the grocer.

The quality of our bread—its taste, texture and the way it kept—surprised us. And friends who tasted it became very excited about it, especially the stone-ground, wholemeal bread. You couldn't buy anything like it in the shops, they said. And it suddenly occurred to us that here perhaps was a means of making money.

We started a little bakery in our kitchen.

It's no easy matter, in these days of Town and Country Planning and Sanitary Inspection and rules and regulations, to start anything, but if the authorities were not exactly enthusiastic about us our customers certainly were. We started with a dozen and within two or three months we had over a hundred. There was a limit to what we could bake and deliver, however, and eventually we found that we should either have to go in for the business properly and operate on a different, impersonal basis, or we should have to devote all our lives, every minute of them, to the baking, and this we did not want to do.

We closed down. But not before we had explored the pleasures of yeast cookery, not before we had tried out and experimented with all sorts of yeast recipes and discovered that the liberal use of yeast in the kitchen opens up a prospect of boundless delights.

At the same time we discovered that a good many people are frightened of baking their own bread. Perhaps they are put off by the idea of all the kneading, or they're mystified by the way yeast works, or they don't

Introduction

think they've got the right sort of oven, or they imagine they will have to go round draught-proofing their kitchen and all that sort of nonsense; whatever the reason, it is apparently a fact that most housewives, in the south of England anyway, do not like the idea of baking their own bread at home.

They don't know what they're missing.

And now that it's no longer a trade secret, so to speak, we would like to explain just how simple and foolproof bread making is.

In the first chapter we're going to concentrate on plain, ordinary bread and how it can be made in the most troublefree way, with the most delicious results.

Once you have made and tasted your own bread it's most unlikely that you will want to return, permanently, to shop bread.

Once you have made a plain bread dough and learned the feel of it, once you have seen it rise and shaped it into loaves, and once you have watched them prove and baked them to your satisfaction, then the whole field of yeast cookery lies waiting for you. While we were baking we tried to introduce a new 'fancy line' every week or so—French bread, Coffee bread, Croissants, Brioches and so on. Everyone knows how delightful these things are to eat but not everyone is aware how easy they are to prepare.

On the whole baking with yeast is easier and more foolproof than making cakes. Yeast is certainly less agitating to work with than baking powder.

And so when we've covered the simple bread recipes

Introduction

we would like to deal with some of the more exciting things that can be made with yeast. We thought it might be useful to have a representative selection of bread and yeast recipes collected together between the covers of one little book.

We have divided these 'fancy' recipes roughly into two sorts—English Tea Breads and Coffee Breads from Abroad. We have included another miscellaneous section for those recipes that don't seem to fit into either category.

The great thing about baking with yeast is the difficulty of failure.

If you find the dough doesn't rise, wait just a little longer; it surely will rise if you haven't forgotten the yeast altogether, and even if you have left it out you can always add it with a little more liquid and flour and set the dough to rise once more. Again, there's no need to worry if you get some of the ingredients weighed out incorrectly. Flour varies in absorbency anyway, and eggs vary in size and fat in oiliness, and so on. You can always add more flour if the dough is too slack, or more liquid if it's too dry.

Really the only thing that can go wrong when baking is—leaving the loaves in the oven and forgetting all about them until they've become nothing more than charred remains.

Before we go any further we would like to say something about flour, and yeast.

Most people who make their own bread begin doing

Introduction

so because they are not satisfied with their baker's wholemeal bread. This may be because he is a bad baker, because of modern steam bakeries, forced rising and the rest, or because of the poor quality of his flour; it may be that his wholemeal bread is not really made from wholemeal flour at all but from a blended and artificial mixture.

Until the introduction of the roller mill in the second half of the nineteenth century, all flour was stone ground. That is to say, the wheat was cleaned, and then ground between stones in one operation. (If you wanted white flour it had to be sieved, or *bolted*. The white flour of the rich, a hundred and fifty years ago, cannot have been very white.)

The roller mill is really a whole series of mills and it doesn't harm the wheat in any way but it enables the miller to separate the flour, the bran, the middlings and the germ. These can of course be blended together again in any proportions you like though normally the bran and the middlings go for stock-feed while the germ is used in many proprietary vitamin preparations.

The white flour from a roller mill, whatever the extraction rate—if the extraction rate is, say, 72, that means 72 parts of flour from 100 parts whole wheat, so the higher the better from a nutritional point of view—and although it may have been enriched with calcium and vitamins, can hardly be of the same food value as plain, wholemeal flour, nothing added, nothing taken away.

But most people, children especially, prefer white bread, And if, in other ways, they eat normal, healthy

Introduction

foods, with a fair amount of green vegetables, meat and milk, they should get a plentiful supply of all the vitamins, proteins and minerals they require. (If you do happen to have a small child who only likes to eat white bread, and hardly any other food at all, then why not give him white bread that's been enriched in the making with milk and eggs and fat?)

All the same, white bread cannot truly qualify as the staff of life. And the taste, not to mention the texture and the keeping qualities, of home-made bread made from stone-ground, wholemeal wheat flour is so much pleasanter, so much nuttier that it really seems unnecessary to go into all the nutritional reasons there may be for preferring it.

We find, moreover, that there is little or no wastage with home-made bread, brown or white, whereas with shop bread we were continually throwing crusts and ends of loaves into the swill bucket.

Unfortunately it is sometimes difficult to obtain supplies of wholemeal flour. You cannot blame the millers for their tendency to give up stone grinding; the public gets what it asks for, and since 1914 something like 96 per cent of all the bread eaten in England has been white.

But there are still quite a few mills that do stone grind wholemeal wheat flour. And you can always buy it at your nearest Health Food Stores, or similar shop. Bought in small 3-lb. bags at a grocer's, however, it will work out very expensive; your bread will cost you considerably more than baker's bread. (For a small baker

Introduction

the profit margin on a loaf of bread, subsidy included, is almost non-existent; he makes his living, if he makes one at all, out of his 'fancies'.) And if you're going to bake any quantity of bread at all—and this applies to all flours—it will be much cheaper to buy it in large quantities, by the ½ or ¼ sack, 10 or 5 stone, direct from a mill.

Try your local millers and you may have a pleasant surprise and find one that still produces stone-ground flour.

Not only will your flour be cheaper like this, it will probably also be fresher and make better bread and cakes. A grocer has to know about a great many things, he is unlikely to be a flour specialist. But that is exactly what a miller is. Flour is his life, and he can and will advise you and supply you with whatever kind of flour you require—for bread, for cakes, for biscuits or for pastry. (Most millers will let you have as little as a stone at a time.) And if you want something rather exotic, like Rye flour, that he can't supply, he will surely put you in touch with a miller who can.

If kept in any dry, mouseproof container (a small dustbin will take 5 stone nicely), the flour, even wholemeal which doesn't keep as well as white, will stay in perfect condition for 3 or 4 months and longer.

As for yeast—there should be no difficulty in obtaining supplies of fresh, compressed baker's yeast, which is the easiest to work with. Any baker, if he is a baker and not just a retailer of factory-made bread, will let you have some—at 2d. the ounce. (A scandalous price, or so it seems to us, for the wholesale price of compressed yeast is 1s. a pound.) And your local Health Food Stores will certainly be able to supply you.

If you can't get fresh, compressed, baker's yeast, the dried yeast that most big grocers stock is perfectly satisfactory for ordinary bread. This should be used in half the quantities recommended for fresh yeast. Dried yeast has rather a strong, beery flavour, though, and cannot be recommended for those 'fancy' recipes which demand a high proportion of yeast to flour. Dried yeast takes a little time to dissolve in warm water and is perhaps not so easy to cream as fresh yeast. Fresh yeast, by the way, will remain in good condition for 10 days or a fortnight if stored in a refrigerator, some distance from the freezing unit—it should be kept wrapped in greaseproof paper or in a covered bowl.

Acknowledgements

When we were running our bakery we browsed our way through a great many cookery books. We should like to mention the following in particular (to the authors of which, alive and dead, our thanks are due, as they started us off on many of our 'lines'.):

Mrs. Beeton's Family Cookery. Ward Lock (no date).

Tante Marie's French Kitchen, translated and adapted by Charlotte Turgeon. Nicholas Kaye, 1950.

The Cereals Section of the Concise Encylopaedia of Gastronomy by Andre L. Simon. Collins, 1952.

The Viennese Cookery Book by Irma Rhode. Lehmann, 1952.

German Cooking by Robin Howe. André Deutsch, 1953.

Italian Cooking by Robin Howe. André Deutsch, 1953.

Jewish Cookery by Leah W. Leonard. André Deutsch, 1951.

Swedish Food, ed. Widdenfeld. Published by Effeltelf, Goteborginduftrir, Sweden, 1948.

We also have to thank *House & Garden* for permission to use material that first appeared in the pages of that magazine.

Acknowledgements

And we are very grateful, too, to James Nutter (Fulbourn) Ltd. who were so kind as to show us round their mill and who told us everything we know about flour and milling.

Weights and Measures

All our recipes are given in pounds and ounces, pints, etc., and our tablespoons are English tablespoons.

But, if anyone wants to go exploring in cookery books it may be useful to know that:

> 1 cup flour is 4 oz.
> 1 cup butter is $\frac{1}{2}$ lb.
> 1 cup milk is 8 fluid oz.

A cup equals half an American pint which is 16 fluid oz. (English pint is 20.)

Two American tablespoons equal one English.

Oven Temperatures

Very hot	440 — 480° F.
Hot	400 — 440° F.
Fairly hot	370 — 400° F.
Moderate	340 — 370° F.
Warm	320 — 340° F.
Cool	280 — 320° F.
Very cool	240 — 280° F.

The Instruction manual with your Gas Cooker will tell you the appropriate settings of the thermostat. On most cookers 7 is about 410° F. (the right temperature to start baking loaves of bread). And to reach this heat most gas ovens will need to be pre-heated for about 15 minutes.

To reach the same heat an electric oven will require 30 minutes' pre-heating.

If you're using a solid-fuel cooker and you're uncertain about the oven temperatures you will find all you need to know in the Instruction Manual. But normally, it's best to start baking in the hottest oven.

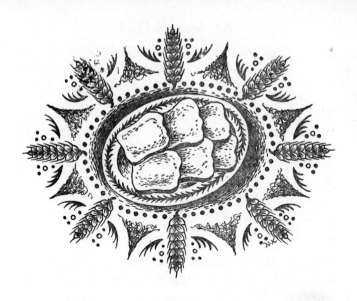

I

Wholemeal Bread
and Rolls; the Simple Bread Recipe and other Plain Bread and Rolls

WHOLEMEAL BREAD—THE SIMPLE BREAD RECIPE

To make four small loaves.

Ingredients: 2½ lb. stone-ground wholemeal flour
      1 oz. fresh yeast, or ½ oz. dried yeast
      2 oz. fat (butter, margarine or lard)
      ½ oz. salt

23

Wholemeal Bread

2 pints warm water—the amount of water required will vary according to the absorbency of the flour

Method. Put the flour in a large bowl. Make a well in the middle. Sprinkle the salt round the edge. Cream the yeast with a little of the water and pour it into the well. Add the fat, warmed and liquid, but not too hot. Pour in the water, but not all at once, sometimes you need more, sometimes less. And mix all the ingredients, lightly and thoroughly, with the fingers; this will make kneading easier.

Kneading. Work through the dough with your fingers and thumbs. Pummel it and punch it and turn it over and over. If you find it easier take the dough out of the bowl and knead it on a board. Go on kneading for about 15 or 20 minutes. What you must aim at is a pleasant, smooth, springy dough of a putty-like consistency. The consistency changes quite suddenly when the dough is ready.

Rising. When the dough is kneaded to your satisfaction, cover the bowl with a damp cloth, and a lid to stop the cloth from drying out, and put it in a warm place to rise. The dough should rise for about 2 hours or until it has doubled in size. In wintertime the linen cupboard is a good place to put it, but in summer the warmth of a draughty kitchen is quite sufficient. The simplest thing, however, is to let the dough rise overnight—in the warmth of your kitchen or living-room or even wrapped

Wholemeal Bread

in an old eiderdown or blanket—and then use it as you want it during the following day.

Shaping. When the dough has risen take it from the bowl and cut it into four and shape into loaves and put them on a lightly floured baking sheet to prove. Or put the dough into well-greased bread tins. (The dough for tins should be a little slacker (wetter) than that for shaped loaves.) Half fill the tins with dough, pressed well down—you don't want ugly folds in your bread.

Proving. You can use the linen cupboard again for the proving. Or you can stand the loaves near a small fire. Or, if you've got a solid fuel cooker or boiler just place them on top of that—on the warm part, not the hot, they don't want too much heat, moderate warmth is all that's required.

Don't worry about draughts. It's heat rather than cold that kills the yeast. A *Croissant* dough will double its size overnight in a refrigerator. And if the dough hasn't been coddled, made to rise too quickly, everything will be all right.

(The man who brought our meat, when we were baking, had been trained as a master baker, and he was scornful of our efforts. 'Draughts will kill anything,' he used to say, looking round at our open doors and windows. But in fact, the draughts never killed anything.)

The loaves should prove for 45 minutes or an hour. You can easily tell when they are ready for the oven; they will be soft and slightly puffy to touch. On the whole it's better to underprove rather than overprove;

loaves that have proved too long will be very bad in texture.

Baking. For the first half hour the bread wants to go in to a hot oven. Then turn the loaves round and let them stay in a moderate or fairly hot oven for another 20 minutes or half an hour. (You should try for conditions resembling the old baker's oven, where the fire was lit inside the oven itself and then raked out when full heat had been raised.)

Of course these oven heats can be varied somewhat according to how you like your bread baked, but 45 minutes is a minimum baking time.

When you finally remove the loaves from the oven put them on a wire tray to cool.

WHOLEMEAL ROLLS

To make about 3 dozen bread rolls.

Ingredients: the same as for wholemeal bread

Method. The same as for the wholemeal bread until you come to the *shaping*. Then all you have to do is to shape the little rolls between the fingers and put them on a lightly floured baking sheet to prove. They need 20 minutes or half an hour to prove and about 15 minutes to bake in a hot oven—it's just as well to turn them round half way through.

These rolls will prove quite nicely on top of a gas oven while it's being pre-heated.

Wholemeal Bread

QUICK WHOLEMEAL BREAD

If you are in a hurry or you suddenly run out of bread you can bake a quick loaf simply by mixing and kneading a rather wet dough (otherwise just the same as for ordinary Wholemeal Bread) and putting it straight into tins and letting it prove for 45 minutes and then putting it in the oven. This bread will be perfectly satisfactory, though it won't be so light as the ordinary bread and it won't keep so well.

(The real advantage of the double rise, the ordinary method, is that you can make as much dough as you like at any one moment and bake when it's convenient. If you're not ready for it, or you can't get it all into the oven in one lot, you can just leave it. The yeast will go on working for a long time.

And it's very pleasant to have fresh rolls for breakfast on Sunday and this is very simple and scarcely any trouble if you make the dough some time on Saturday afternoon or evening.)

WHITE BREAD

To make 4 small loaves.

Ingredients: 2½ lb. white flour
1 oz. fresh yeast, or ½ oz. dried
2 oz. fat (butter, margarine or lard)
½ oz. salt
About 1½ pints warm water

Wholemeal Bread

Method. The simple bread recipe, as for Wholemeal Bread. WHITE ROLLS and QUICK WHITE BREAD can be made in exactly the same way as the wholemeal, only substituting white flour for wholemeal and using rather less water.

HALF-AND-HALF BREAD makes a pleasant change

To make 4 small loaves.

Ingredients: 1½ lb. white flour
    1 lb. wholemeal flour
    1 oz. fresh yeast or ½ oz. dried
    2 oz. fat
    ½ oz. salt
    1½ pints warm water (approx.)

Method. The simple bread recipe, as for Wholemeal Bread.

VIENNA BREAD

To make 4 small loaves.

Ingredients: 2½ lb. white flour
    1 oz. fresh yeast, or ½ oz. dried
    4 oz. butter or margarine
    ½ oz. salt
    1 pint warm milk, plus warm water as required

Method. The simple bread recipe, as for Wholemeal

Wholemeal Bread

Bread. Special attention can be paid to the shaping of the loaves and the crusts should be painted with rich milk when the loaves are turned round.

BRIDGE ROLLS

To make about 3 dozen bridge rolls.

Ingredients: 2½ lb. white flour
              1 oz. fresh yeast or ½ oz. dried
              4 oz. butter or margarine
              ½ oz. salt
              2 eggs
              1 pint warm milk, plus water if required

Method. The simple bread recipe, as for Wholemeal rolls. The eggs should be whisked up with the milk before adding to the flour. The rolls should be shaped into little sausages and painted with milk immediately before baking.

RYE BREAD

There are many different types of Rye bread. Nearly every Continental country has its own varieties. The nutritive value of rye is almost as great as wheat, and indeed rye flour contains some valuable food elements that wheat lacks.

If you want Rye flour ask your local miller if he knows who can supply you. It is normally milled in three grades, ranging from a fine, light Rye flour to Wholemeal.

Wholemeal Bread

LIGHT RYE BREAD

Using the simple bread recipe (as for Wholemeal Bread) and a 50-50 mixture of light Rye flour and ordinary white wheat flour you can produce a pleasant enough Rye loaf. But apart from a slight stickiness in texture there will be little to distinguish this from ordinary bread.

To obtain the essential Rye flavour you must use a sour dough.

SOUR DOUGH PASTE

A few days before you want to make your bread mix two or three tablespoonfuls of Rye flour with a little warm milk and make a paste. Leave this covered in a bowl in the warmth of your kitchen until it smells pleasantly sour.

Then you are ready to make your Rye bread. The following method is most satisfactory. The flour proportions can of course be varied according to individual taste. (You can use only Rye flour.)

SOUR RYE BREAD

To make 4 small loaves.

Ingredients: 1½ lb. Wholemeal Rye
1 lb. plain white flour (Wheat)
½ oz. salt
4 oz. fat

Wholemeal Bread

1 pint warm milk, and warm water as required (sour milk is better)
½oz. fresh yeast or ¼ oz. dried
And the Sour Dough Paste

Strictly speaking the yeast is unnecessary. The Sour Dough Paste should be perfectly satisfactory as a leavening agent, but the yeast saves anxiety.

Method. Put all the flour and the salt in a large bowl and mix well together. Make a well and pour in the Sour Dough Paste and the fat, warmed and liquid but not too hot. Add the yeast, creamed in a little of the milk. And then the kneading, the rising and the proving are the same as for the simple bread recipe (Wholemeal Bread) except that it is perhaps easier to make tin loaves. (As far as rising and proving is concerned Rye is a little tricky, and in our experience Rye flour varies more from sack to sack than Wheat.)

Baking. This Rye bread should go into a fairly hot oven for half an hour. Then, when turning it round, paint the crust with milk or salt water, and bake in a moderate to cool oven for at least another hour and a half.

If you put a small ball of the dough in a bowl, cover it with milk and put it on one side, you will have a Sour Dough Paste all ready for the next baking. This paste will keep for about a fortnight.

QUICK RYE BREAD

The Sour Rye makes as satisfactory a quick bread as any we have tried. And the dough requires very little

Wholemeal Bread

kneading—5 minutes are often enough, or until you've got a nice, smooth dough. Unfortunately it does take rather a long time to prove and bake, and you can't hurry Rye bread—if it's baked too soon or too fast then it tends to crack and split and is not very satisfactory.

FRENCH BREAD

To make 4 small loaves (or *flutes*).

Stage 1. Ingredients: 1 lb. white flour
1 oz. fresh yeast
½ pint warm water

Method. Put the flour in a bowl. Make a well. Cream the yeast very carefully and thoroughly with some of the water and pour it into the well. Add the rest of the water. Mix and knead until all the water has been absorbed. Then cover the bowl with a dry cloth and put it in a warm place to rise for about 3 hours—or overnight.

Stage 2. Ingredients: 1 lb. flour
½ oz. salt
½ pint warm water
And the dough you've already made

Method. Dissolve the salt in the water and pour it all over the dough, which will have a crusty skin on it. Mix up well until you have got rid of the skin. Then gradually add the flour and knead for as long as you like. The longer the better, for the object is to make the dough as light as possible, but 10 or 15 minutes will be sufficient.

Wholemeal Bread

Then lift the dough and slap it down into the bowl, again and again; go on doing this for a few minutes, as long as you can stand it! Cover the bowl with a damp cloth and put it back in a warm place to rise for at least 2 hours.

Stage 3. Method. Divide the dough into 4 equal portions. Roll each piece into a ball and leave for 15 minutes covered with a dry cloth, on a floured board.

Now spread a clean teacloth on a baking sheet and sprinkle it liberally with flour.

When the 15 minutes are up shape each ball into a long strand sausage by rolling and pulling, as long and as thin a strand as your baking sheet will take comfortably. Then lay the loaves you have thus fashioned on the cloth, pulling the cloth well up between the loaves and at each side, to prevent the bread from expanding outwards. Cover the whole with another cloth and allow to prove in moderate warmth for 1 hour.

Then roll the loaves very gently off the cloth, one by one, on to the baking sheet. Touch them as little as possible—they shouldn't have stuck to the cloth if it was well floured, but if they have a wooden spoon is better than fingers for removing them.

Make two or three shallow cuts on each loaf with a very sharp knife (a razor-blade knife is best) and bake in a hot oven for about 1 hour. The oven door should not be opened for the first half hour, and then they'll probably need turning and the crusts can be painted with melted butter or margarine or milk.

c

Wholemeal Bread

To make 2 medium-sized loaves.

Ingredients: 2 lb. flour. (White or Wholemeal)
        ½ oz. salt
        2 teaspoons bicarbonate of soda and 2 of cream of tartar—or 1 oz. baking powder
        2 oz. melted butter or margarine
        1 pint milk, preferably sour or buttermilk

Method. Put the flour and the salt and the raising agents in a bowl and mix very thoroughly. Make a well and pour in the milk and the melted fat. Mix quickly, lightly and carefully. Divide the dough into two and shape into loaves and place on a floured baking sheet. Brush over with milk and bake in a hot oven for about 45 minutes.

2

Gilding the Loaf

One of the secrets of making supremely edible-looking and appetizing bread is the shape and finish of the loaves and rolls.

You shape the loaves before you put them out to prove.

To make a cottage loaf: roll one large ball of dough and put it on the baking sheet. Roll a smaller ball (about $\frac{1}{3}$ the size of the first) and place that on top of the first and press a floury finger right down through the middle of both.

To make a plait: divide the dough into 3, 5 or 7 equal portions. Roll each of these between fingers and hands until they are long thin strands, then plait them together just as if you were plaiting a rope or a girl's hair. It's generally best to plait loosely rather than tightly.

To make a bun twist: simply roll out the dough into a long sausage and tie the ends loosely together—as if tying a knot.

To make a Viennese Twist: roll out the dough into a tapering strand, about 2 feet long, as thick as your fist one end, and as thin as you like at the other. Then roll it up into a coil, starting from the thick end so that the thinner portions form graduated steps. Finally twist the tail over the top and smooth the whole thing into a nice oval.

For buns and muffins, etc.: it's much easier to roll out the dough flat on a floured board and cut them out with a sharp knife or a tumbler than to pull handfuls of dough out of the bowl and shape between the fingers.

The Finish. If you want your plain loaves to have a gleaming, brown crust paint them with rich milk or cream before putting them in the oven (or when you turn them round). Painted with beaten egg they will

Gilding the Loaf

have a darker crust, almost black. If you want them to have a crisp, crunchy crust, paint them with melted butter or margarine.

And if you want your sweet loaves and buns to shine in a most beautiful and sticky way, paint them with a thick milk and sugar syrup as soon as they come out of the oven. The difference this makes to the look of a fruit loaf is quite extraordinary.

3

English Tea Breads

CURRENT BREAD (FRUIT LOAF)

To make 2 medium-sized loaves.

Ingredients: 1½ lb. white flour
1 oz. fresh yeast
4 oz. butter or margarine
4 oz. sugar
Pinch of salt
½ pint warm milk

English Tea Breads

4 oz. sultanas
4 oz. currants
2 oz. candied peel

Method. Put the flour in a large bowl. Mix in the sugar
and the salt. Make a well. Pour in the yeast, creamed in
a litte of the milk. Add the butter, warmed and liquid
but not too hot, and the rest of the milk. Knead
thoroughly, adding warm water if required, and cover
with a damp cloth and put in a warm place to rise for
1½ hours or until the dough has doubled in size. Then
knock the dough down and knead in the fruit and shape
into loaves (or use tins, half filled with the dough,
pressed well down). Prove for 45 minutes and bake for
30 to 45 minutes in a moderate to fairly hot oven,
turning the loaves round after the first 20 minutes.
Paint the loaves with a thick milk and sugar syrup as
soon as you have taken them from the oven.

This same dough makes excellent CURRANT BUNS.
And many kinds of fruit bread can be made by varying
the fruit (try dates and raisins, for example) and the
flour. A SULTANA LOAF, made entirely with Wholemeal
flour, makes very pleasant eating.

MALT BREAD

To make 2 medium-sized loaves.

Ingredients: 1 lb. stone-ground Wholemeal flour
¼ lb. white flour
Pinch of salt

English Tea Breads

1 oz. fresh yeast
About ¾ pint warm water
2 oz. butter or margarine
2 tablespoons black treacle
2 tablespoons extract of malt
2 oz. sultanas (if you like)

Method. Put the flour and the salt in a large bowl and mix. Make a well. Pour in the yeast, creamed in a little of the water. Add the treacle, the malt extract, the butter, warmed and liquid but not too hot, and the water (as required). Knead until the dough is of even texture and all the malt and treacle have been blended in. Cover with a damp cloth and leave to rise in a warm place for 2 hours or until the dough has doubled in size. Put the dough into tins, pressed well down, and prove for 45 minutes. Bake in a moderate oven for 45 minutes, turning the loaves round after the first 25 minutes. Paint the loaves with a thick milk and sugar syrup as soon as you have taken them from the oven and removed them from their tins.

Malt Bread keeps very well, even improves after 2 or 3 days. And this mixture makes very good MALT BUNS, too.

OATMEAL BREAD

To make 2 small loaves.

Ingredients: ½ lb. medium oatmeal
¾ pint milk
½ oz. fresh yeast

2 oz. butter or margarine
4 teaspoons salt
And about ½ lb. flour (white or wholemeal)

Method. Put the oatmeal in a large bowl. Pour on the milk and leave to soak for at least 2 hours.

Then add the yeast, creamed in a very little warm water, the fat, warmed and liquid but not too hot, the salt and the flour—just as much as you need to make a nice, smooth dough—and knead thoroughly.

Cover the bowl with a damp cloth and leave the dough to rise in a warm place for about 1½ hours or until the dough has doubled in size. Then shape into loaves and prove for about 45 minutes. Bake in a hot oven for 30 minutes. Then turn the loaves round and finish them off in a moderate to cool oven for another 20 or 30 minutes.

This oatmeal dough makes the most delicious OATMEAL BUNS.

WALNUT BREAD

To make 2 medium-sized loaves.

Ingredients: 1 lb. white flour
½ lb. wholemeal flour
½ oz. salt
1 oz. sugar
4 oz. butter or margarine
1 oz. fresh yeast
¾ pint warm milk, plus water if required
4 oz. walnut halves

Method. Put the flour, the sugar and the salt in a large bowl and mix thoroughly. Make a well. Pour in the yeast, creamed in a little of the milk, and the fat, warmed and liquid but not too hot, and the rest of the milk. Knead, adding warm water if required Cover with a damp cloth and leave to rise in a warm place for $1\frac{1}{2}$ hours or until the dough has doubled in size. Knock down the dough and knead in the walnut halves until they are evenly distributed throughout. Shape into loaves and prove for 45 minutes. Bake for 30 minutes in a hot oven, then turn the loaves round and finish them off in a moderate one for another 20 or 25 minutes.

BATH BUNS

To make about 18 medium-sized buns.

Ingredients: 1 lb. white flour
4 oz. butter or margarine
1 oz. fresh yeast
$\frac{1}{8}$ pint milk
4 oz. sugar
3 eggs
Small pinch of salt
4 oz. sultanas
2 oz. candied peel
A small quantity of crushed candy sugar, and
1 egg beaten with a tablespoonful of milk

Method. Break the eggs into a bowl. Add the milk and the butter, warmed and liquid but not hot, and whisk thoroughly.

English Tea Breads

Put the flour, the sugar and the salt in a large bowl and mix. Make a well. Pour in the yeast, creamed in a little warm water. Pour in the milk-butter-eggs mixture, and knead thoroughly. Cover the bowl with a damp cloth and leave to rise in a warm place for 2 hours or until the dough has doubled in size. Then beat the dough down and add the fruit and knead for a minute or two until evenly distributed. Shape into oval buns and prove on a floured baking sheet for 45 minutes. Brush them over with the egg and milk and powder them with the crushed candy sugar and bake in a fairly hot oven for about 30 minutes.

MUFFINS

To make 18 small muffins.

Ingredients: 1 lb. flour
        ½ pint milk
        ½ oz. fresh yeast
        1 egg
        1 teaspoonful salt
        1 oz. butter or margarine

Method. Break the egg into a bowl. Add the milk and the butter, warmed and liquid but not too hot, and whisk.

Put the flour and the salt into a large bowl. Make a well and pour in the yeast, creamed in a little warm water. Add the butter-egg-milk mixture. Knead thoroughly, adding more flour or water as required, to make a soft dough that is not too sticky. Cover the bowl with a damp cloth and leave to rise in a warm place for about 1½ hours or until the dough has doubled in size.

Roll out the dough to a ½-inch thickness on a floured board. You will probably need more flour to sprinkle on the board and the dough to stop it from sticking. Cut the muffins out with a large tumbler. Punch any remains together and roll out and cut again until all the dough has been used.

The muffins should be baked right away on a griddle, being turned as soon as they're nicely browned on the bottom side. But if you've no griddle they will turn out very well if baked, without proving, on a baking sheet in a very hot oven with plenty of bottom heat and turned over after 6 or 7 minutes, and then given another 6 or 7 minutes.

CHELSEA BUNS

To make 18 buns.

Ingredients: 1 lb. white flour (scant)
         4 oz. butter or margarine
         4 oz. granulated sugar
         1 oz. fresh yeast
         The zest of 1 lemon
         2 eggs
         4 oz. currants
         About ⅛ pint milk
         And 2 or 3 tablespoons of thick milk and
           sugar syrup

English Tea Breads

Method. Break the eggs into a bowl. Add the milk and half the butter (liquid and cool) and whisk thoroughly.

Put the flour in a bowl with half the sugar and mix. Make a well. Pour in the yeast, creamed in a little warm water. Add the milk-eggs-butter mixture and the zest of one lemon (and more flour or milk as required to make a smooth, soft dough) and knead. Cover with a damp cloth and leave to rise in a warm place for 1½ hours or until the dough has doubled in size.

Then roll out the dough on a floured board into a thin strip about ¼-inch thick and about 3 times as long as it's wide. Spread the rest of the butter (softened, but not melted) over it. And sprinkle the currants and the rest of the sugar over the butter. Fold in the ends of the strip to make a square and roll out the other way into a strip the same size. Fold in the ends to make a square once more and then roll up the square like a Swiss Roll. Cut into thick slices and put them on their sides, almost touching, on a floured baking sheet. Let them prove for 30 minutes and then bake them for 20 to 30 minutes in a fairly hot oven. Brush them heavily with the milk and sugar syrup when you have removed them from the oven.

CORNISH SPLITS

To make about 2 dozen.

Ingredients: ¼ pint milk
1 oz. fresh yeast
4 oz. butter or margarine

1 teaspoon salt
1 teaspoon sugar
1 lb. white flour

Method. Warm the milk and dissolve the yeast in it. Add the sugar and salt and a few spoonfuls of flour, and stir. Leave to rise in a warm place until you can see that the yeast is working (bubbling).

Then add the flour and the butter, warmed and liquid but not too hot, and warm water, if required, to make a soft, smooth dough. Knead well. Cover with a damp cloth and leave to rise in a warm place for 1½ hours or until the dough has doubled in size.

Shape into small balls (about the size of a tangerine). Flatten the tops and bake, without proving, for about 20 minutes in a hot oven until golden brown.

Serve cold, split open, with clotted cream and strawberry jam.

TEA CAKES

1. *Plain Tea Cakes (Sally Lunns)*
   To make 4 large cakes.

Ingredients: 1 lb. white flour
¼ pint milk
4 oz. butter or margarine
1 oz. sugar
Large pinch of salt
1 egg
1 oz. yeast

English Tea Breads

Method. Break the egg into a bowl and whisk in the milk and the butter, warmed and liquid but not too hot.

Put the flour in a large bowl with the sugar and the salt and mix. Make a well. Pour in the yeast, creamed in a little warm water. Add the milk-fat-egg mixture and knead thoroughly. Cover the bowl with a damp cloth and leave to rise in a warm place for 1½ hours until the dough has doubled in size.

Then beat the dough down and knead briskly for a few minutes. Roll out the dough on a floured board to a thickness of about ½ inch. Cut the cakes out with an up-turned pudding basin and a knife. Let them prove on a floured baking sheet for 30 minutes.

With a sharp knife make four shallow cuts from the centre in each cake, to divide them into portions. And bake for about 20 minutes in a hot oven, turning them round after the first 10 minutes, until nicely browned. The cakes can be glazed by painting with a milk and sugar syrup as soon as they come out of the oven.

Ideally, these cakes should be made just in time for tea and sliced open as soon as they come out of the oven and buttered thickly and served hot.

They toast up very well.

2. *Fruit Tea Cakes*

These can be made in exactly the same way as the Sally Lunns, only when you knock the dough down after it has risen for the first time, knead in 2 oz. currants, 2 oz. sultanas and 2 oz. of candied peel.

SPICE BUNS (WIGS)

To make 2 dozen wigs.

Ingredients: 1 lb. flour
2 oz. butter or margarine
2 oz. sugar
1 teaspoonful mixed spice
¼ oz. caraway seeds
½ oz. fresh yeast
½ pint milk
Pinch of salt

Method. Melt the fat and allow it to cool.

Put the flour, the mixed spice, the caraway seeds, the sugar and the salt in a bowl and mix. Make a well. Pour in the yeast, creamed in a little warm water, and the milk. Knead thoroughly, adding more milk or flour if required to make a nice, smooth, soft dough. Roll out the dough on a floured board and cut into wedge-shaped buns. Put them on a floured baking sheet to prove for 30 minutes. Bake them for about 20 minutes in a hot oven, turning them round at half time.

(According to the *Encyclopaedia of Gastronomy*, 'A wigg was a wedge and these (Wigs) are wedge-shaped cakes'.)

SPICE BREAD

To make 2 small loaves.

Ingredients: 1 lb. flour
1 oz. yeast

English Tea Breads

2 oz. butter or margarine
Pinch of salt
2 oz. sugar
2 teaspoons mixed spice
2 oz. sultanas
2 oz. currants
1 oz. candied peel
About ½ pint milk

Method. Put the flour, the salt and the sugar in a large bowl and mix. Make a well. Pour in the yeast, creamed in a little of the milk. Add the spice, the rest of the milk and the butter, warmed and liquid but not too hot. Knead thoroughly. Cover the bowl with a damp cloth and leave to rise in a warm place for 1½ hours or until the dough has doubled itself.

Knock the dough down and knead in the fruit until it is all evenly distributed through the dough.

Shape the loaves and prove for 30 to 45 minutes. Bake for 30 to 45 minutes in a moderate or fairly hot oven, turning the loaves round at half time.

HOT CROSS BUNS

To make about 18 medium-sized buns.

Ingredients: 1 lb. flour
1 oz. yeast
2 oz. butter or margarine
2 oz. moist sugar
2 large teaspoons mixed spice

D

49

English Tea Breads

(To make the best ever Hot Cross Buns,
    grind your own spice fresh)

1 egg
4 oz. currants
2 oz. candied peel
And about ½ pint milk

Method. If you want the buns for Good Friday breakfast
make the dough some time on Thursday afternoon or
evening.

Put the flour, the sugar, the salt and the spice in a
large bowl and mix. Make a well. Pour in the yeast,
creamed in a little of the milk. Add the egg and the
butter, warmed and liquid but not too hot. Knead to a
nice, clean, smooth dough (on the stiff side), using as
much milk as you require. Then add the fruit and knead
it evenly through the dough. Cover the bowl with a
damp cloth and leave to rise overnight in the warmth
of your kitchen (or for 2 hours until the dough has
doubled itself).

Knock the dough down and shape the buns and set
them on a baking tray to prove for about 30 minutes.
Mark the crosses on them with a paper knife or a blunt
pointed pencil and bake in a hot oven for about 15
minutes (turning them round as necessary).

Brush them over with a thick milk and sugar syrup
when they come from the oven, to glaze them.

English Tea Breads

To make 1 good-sized cake.

Ingredients: ¾ lb. flour
 ¼ pint milk
 2 oz. butter or margarine
 1 oz. fresh yeast
 2 eggs
 4 oz. moist sugar
 6 oz. currants
 2 oz. candied peel

Method. Melt the butter and put it in a bowl and allow to cool. Break in the eggs and pour in the milk and whisk to a froth.

Put the flour and sugar in a large bowl and mix. Make a well. Pour in the yeast, creamed in a very little warm water. Add the milk-butter-eggs mixture, and knead until you've made a nice smooth, soft dough. Then cover the bowl with a damp cloth and leave to rise in a warm place for at least 1½ hours, or until the dough has doubled itself.

Now add the fruit and knead well to make sure it's evenly distributed.

Line a cake tin with greasepaper and put in the dough. Let it prove for ½ hour. Bake for 30 minutes in a hot oven, then for about 1 hour in a moderate to cool oven.

DOUGHNUTS

(There are a whole host of doughnuts, English, American and Continental, but the following is a good, basic recipe.)

To make about 2 dozen medium-sized doughnuts.

Ingredients: ¾ lb. flour

1 oz. yeast

¼ pint warm milk

2 oz. butter or margarine, melted but cool

1 small egg

2 oz. sugar

Pinch of salt

Jam (raspberry?) and a little milk or egg for sealing—if you want to fill them

Some kitchen paper to lay them on for draining will be needed. And a quantity of castor sugar to roll them in

Method. Dissolve the yeast in the warm milk. Beat in an ounce or two of the flour and leave covered in a warm place for 30 minutes.

Beat the egg, the sugar, the salt and the melted butter together with a whisk.

Join the two mixtures together and beat with the whisk. Then slap the rest of the flour gradually in with the fingers and hand. (A little more or a little less flour may be required—to make a soft, smooth dough, but not a sticky one.)

English Tea Breads

Cover with a damp cloth and leave to rise in a warm place for at least 1 hour.

Knock the dough down and knead for a few minutes.

Then, if you want to make filled doughnuts, roll little balls of the dough between the fingers. Flatten them with a rolling pin on a floured board. Put a teaspoonful of jam in the middle and fold up, sealing the edges with milk or egg.

If you want to make ring doughnuts, roll the dough out on the floured board and cut them out with a doughnut cutter. If you have no cutter you can use an upturned egg cup and a tumbler.

Or you can make doughnuts of whatever shape you fancy. The important thing to remember, though, is that they will swell up enormously as soon as they hit the fat in the frying pan so that all doughnuts must be made much smaller than one would at first imagine.

Set them to prove on a floured board or baking sheet, covered with a cloth, for about 15 minutes.

Fry them in deep boiling fat, turning them over as they get nicely browned on the underside. (They take about 7 or 8 minutes all together.)

Remove them and put them on paper to drain. Then roll them in the castor sugar. And the fresher—the warmer, almost—you serve them the better.

4

Coffee Breads from Abroad

CROISSANTS (France)

To make about 2 dozen.

Ingredients: ¼ pint scalded milk
1 oz. butter or margarine
1 heaped teaspoon salt
1½ tablespoons sugar
1 oz. fresh yeast dissolved in a little warm water
12 oz. flour (more or less)
4 oz. butter or margarine
1 egg yolk, beaten with a little milk

Coffee Breads from Abroad

Method. Stage 1. Put the 1 oz. margarine or butter and the salt and sugar in a bowl. Pour the milk over, hot enough to melt the fat. Leave to cool to lukewarm and then add the dissolved yeast and stir. Add the flour, gradually, and knead until the dough is soft, smooth and elastic. Cover the bowl with a damp cloth and put in a warm place to rise for two hours, or until the dough has doubled in size.

Stage 2. Knock the dough down and put it in the refrigerator, or in a cold place, to chill thoroughly. Meanwhile wash the 4 oz. butter or margarine by putting it in a large bowl of cold water and squeezing it between fingers until it is all soft and nicely spreadable.

Stage 3. When the dough is chilled (after about 30 minutes in the frig or 1 hour in the cold) roll it out on a floured board into a strip three times as long as it's wide. Spread the washed butter or margarine evenly over the strip and fold in the ends to form a square. Roll it out into another strip the same size—the other way—and fold in the ends to form a square and put it back in the frig or in the cold place, to chill thoroughly again. Roll it out and fold twice more, at intervals of 30 minutes, and then leave it in the refrigerator or in the cold for an hour at the very least—or overnight, if you want croissants for breakfast. The dough will then be ready for shaping and baking.

Stage 4. Shaping. Roll the dough out on a floured board to ¼ inch thickness. Cut into 4-inch squares. Divide each square into 2 triangles. Roll each triangle up, starting at the longest base and rolling towards the apex, so that the pointed end is in the centre and underneath the roll. Shape into crescents and place on a lightly floured baking sheet.

Stage 5. Baking. Brush the croissants with the beaten egg yolk and milk and bake for 10 to 15 minutes (without proving) in a fairly hot or hot oven.

YEAST PUFF PASTE

To make a small quantity.

Ingredients: 1 oz. fresh yeast
$\frac{1}{4}$ pint lukewarm milk
2 oz. sugar
2 oz. butter or margarine, melted but cool
2 eggs, well beaten
Pinch of salt
$\frac{3}{4}$ lb. flour
$\frac{1}{2}$ lb. butter for spreading

Method. Dissolve the yeast in the milk. Add the sugar and salt and stir. Add enough flour to make a thin paste. Leave to rise in a warm place for 30 minutes or so.

Beat the melted butter with the eggs. Beat in the yeast—flour mixture. Gradually add the rest of the flour, slapping it in with the fingers. This must be a soft, smooth, elastic dough.

Leave to rise under a cloth in a warm place until doubled in size ($1\frac{1}{2}$ hours).

Wash the $\frac{1}{2}$ lb. butter by squeezing it between the fingers in a bowl of cold water until it is all soft and nicely spreadable. Then divide the butter in half and leave it in a bowl of cold water until you are ready for it.

Knock the dough together and roll it out on a floured board into a strip about ¼-inch thick and about three times as long as it's wide.

Shake one half of the butter dry and spread it over the centre third of the strip. Pull one end over, patting it down at the edges, and spread the rest of the butter over that. Pull the remaining end over and pat down the edges. Roll the dough out the other way into strip the same size. Fold the ends in to make a square. Chill for half an hour in the refrigerator or for an hour in a cold place.

Roll it out again and fold in. Repeat this twice more at intervals of thirty minutes (rather longer if you have no refrigerator). Then allow the dough to rise for half an hour or so in moderate warmth.

The Yeast Puff Paste dough is ready for use.

DANISH PASTRY can be made with this dough

Roll out the dough on a floured board to ¼-inch thickness. Cut into shapes, as you fancy, fill with dried fruit, nuts, preserves, jam, etc.

Brush with a mixture of melted butter, egg and milk and bake (without proving) in a moderate oven for about 30 minutes.

When you take the pastries out of the oven you can either ice them or dust them with icing sugar.

Coffee Breads from Abroad

SWEET CROISSANTS can be made with this dough

Roll out the dough to a thickness of $\frac{1}{4}$ inch on a floured board. Cut into 4-inch squares. Divide the squares into triangles and roll up as for Croissants. Brush with egg and milk and bake without proving for about 30 minutes in a moderate oven.

KOLATSCHEN (Bohemia) can be made with this dough

Roll out the dough on a floured board to $\frac{1}{4}$-inch thickness. Cut into small squares or circles according to fancy. Press down with your thumb in the centre of each so as to make a little indentation and fill the hole with jam, fruit, poppy seeds, nuts, sour milk cheese, whatever you like. Brush with melted butter, egg-and-milk mixture and bake, without proving, in a moderate or fairly hot oven for about 30 minutes. Dust with icing sugar.

And with this dough, of course, you can also make most of the things you can make with Puff Pastry. It is difficult to be over-enthusiastic about YEAST PUFF PASTE.

SWEET CROISSANTS (Austria)

To make about 2 dozen.

Ingredients: 1 oz. fresh yeast
$\frac{1}{4}$ pint lukewarm milk (scant)
2 oz. sugar

Coffee Breads from Abroad

Pinch of salt
4 oz. butter or margarine
4 eggs
1 lb. flour (a little more may be needed)
The zest of 2 lemons
Egg and water, beaten, for brushing

Method. Dissolve the yeast in the milk. Add the sugar and salt and stir. Leave for a few minutes.

Melt the butter and allow to cool. Beat the eggs in with the butter, one after the other. Whisk till good and frothy.

Prepare the lemon zest.

Combine the yeast mixture, the lemon zest and the egg and butter mixture. Whisk. Gradually add the flour, slapping it in with the fingers, and knead until you have a soft, smooth dough.

Roll out the dough to a $\frac{1}{4}$-inch thickness on a floured board. Cut into 4-inch squares. Divide the squares into triangles and roll up as for ordinary croissants.

Prove on a lightly floured baking sheet for about 30 minutes. You don't want them to rise too much. Brush with the beaten egg and water and bake for 20 minutes in a fairly hot oven.

These sweet Croissants can be filled with jam or preserves if you like.

BRIOCHE (1)

To make about 18, in Castle Pudding tins.

Ingredients: 2 oz. flour
1 oz. fresh yeast
2 tablespoonfuls warm water
6 oz. flour
3 eggs
6 oz. melted butter (cool)
1 teaspoon salt
1 tablespoon sugar

Method. Cream the yeast in the warm water and mix with 2 oz. flour. Put the little ball of dough into a bowl of warm water—where it will very quickly double in size and form a sponge on top of the water.

Put the 6 oz. flour into a bowl and beat in the 3 eggs with your fingers. If too dry to beat add a little water. Beat for 5 or 10 minutes. Add the butter, salt and sugar and beat some more. Remove the yeast sponge from the water and mix it in with the batter. When everything seems truly blended together cover with a damp cloth and put in a warm place to rise for 2 or 3 hours. Then knock the dough down and leave in a cool place overnight.

In the morning the dough must be treated gently to keep the brioches as light as possible.

The dough can be baked as a cake in a ring mould, or in proper brioche tins (!) or in castle pudding tins. Half fill the tins with the dough, and allow to prove for

Coffee Breads from Abroad

30 minutes. Bake in a hot oven; a ring loaf for about 30 minutes, castle pudding brioches for 15 or 20 minutes. If, after 10 or 15 minutes, the tops seem to be burning, you can either cover them with paper or bake a little longer at lower heat. If you're not sure whether they're baked or not you can always test them with a needle—like a cake.

BRIOCHE (2)

To make about 15 in Castle Pudding tins.

Ingredients: ½ lb. flour
4 oz. butter or margarine
2 eggs
1 oz. yeast
1 teaspoon brandy
⅓ pint water
Pinch salt
Teaspoon sugar

Method. Crumble the yeast and mix it thoroughly (dry) with the flour in a bowl. Add the eggs, the sugar and the salt, and mix some more. Then pour in the butter, warmed and liquid but not too hot, and the water, to make a thick batter. Beat with a large spoon or with the fingers for 10 or 15 minutes or until the mixture begins to bubble. Stir in the brandy. Cover the bowl with a damp cloth and leave to rise in a warm place for at least 2 hours, or overnight.

Fill castle pudding tins (or proper brioche tins) half

full with the mixture and bake (without proving), in a hot oven for about 15 minutes.

SWEET BRIOCHE—PANETTONE (Italy)

To make 1 medium-sized cake or about a dozen small ones.

Ingredients: Stage 1. 6 oz. flour
1 oz. yeast
¼ pint warm milk

Method. Cream the yeast in a little of the milk. Put the flour in a bowl. Make a well and pour in the yeast and the rest of the milk. Mix carefully and leave to rise in a warm place for 1½ hours.

Ingredients: Stage 2. 6 oz. flour
2 oz. melted butter
3 egg yolks
Pinch of salt
2 oz. sugar
3 oz. stoned raisins
2 oz. candied peel
Zest of 1 lemon
1 egg, beaten, for brushing

Method. Put this flour in another bowl and mix in the salt and the sugar. Then beat in the egg yolks and the fat with the fingers until the whole is nicely yellow. Now add the yeast dough (made in stage 1) and knead thoroughly. You want a good stiff dough so if it's too wet add a little flour.

Lastly, add the raisins, the candied peel and the lemon zest, and knead until the fruit is evenly distributed through the dough.

Cover with a damp cloth and leave to rise overnight or until doubled in size (2 hours). Prove for 30 minutes in patty pans or on a well-greased baking sheet. And brush with beaten egg and bake for 10 to 15 minutes in a hot oven, then a further 10 or 15 minutes in a moderate oven.

APPLE CAKE—APFELKUCHEN (Germany)

To make 2 small cakes.

Ingredients: 1 oz. fresh yeast
$\frac{1}{8}$ pint warm milk
$\frac{1}{2}$ lb. flour.
1 oz. butter or margarine
Zest of 1 lemon
1 oz. sugar
1 egg
Pinch of salt
Apples as required
Breadcrumbs or sugar for dredging and cinnamon and sugar for sprinkling over

Method. Dissolve the yeast in the warm milk. Mix in a little of the flour, enough to make a thin paste, and leave to stand in a warm place for 30 minutes.

Add the rest of the flour, the butter (warmed and liquid but not too hot), the lemon zest, the sugar and the salt.

Coffee Breads from Abroad

Knead until the dough is quite smooth. Cover with a cloth and leave to rise for at least 1½ hours or until the dough has doubled in size.

Roll out on to well-greased tins (sponge cake tins are excellent for these cakes). Dredge with sugar or breadcrumbs. Peel apples, as required, and slice them thinly and arrange the slices prettily, overlapping, so as to cover the cake. Sprinkle with cinnamon and sugar and bake in a fairly hot oven for 15 to 20 minutes.

This same dough makes very good cakes with plums, prunes, dried apricots, what you will.

MILK STEAM CAKE (France)

To make 1 medium-sized cake.

Ingredients: 2 oz. butter or margarine
⅛ pint warm milk
1 oz. fresh yeast
1 oz. sugar
Pinch of salt
2 egg yolks
8 oz. flour
To pour over: ¼ pint milk and 1 oz. sugar
And some cinnamon and sugar

Method. Melt the butter. Pour it into a bowl and let it cool to lukewarm. Add the egg yolks, the sugar and the salt and the yeast, dissolved in the warm milk. Stir and mix until the sugar is dissolved.

Add the flour andknead until the dough is creamy

and smooth. Then roll into a long sausage. Cut into ½-inch slices and put them into a well-greased baking pan. Cover the pan and let the cake rise for 45 minutes or until doubled in size. Then bake for about 15 or 20 minutes in a moderate or fairly hot oven, until light brown.

Meanwhile heat the ¼ pint milk and stir in the sugar.

Remove the cake from the oven as soon as it is nicely golden brown and pour over the hot milk and sugar. It will soak in immediately and the cake should rise high.

Sprinkle with the sugar and cinnamon and serve.

SAVARIN CAKE (France)

To make 1 small cake.

Ingredients: 1 oz. yeast
⅛ pint milk, warmed
4 oz. flour
2 eggs
Pinch of salt
1 heaped teaspoon sugar
2 oz. butter
Small quantity of finely chopped almonds
2 tablespoons water, 2 oz. sugar and 1 tablespoon rum—for the icing syrup
Whole blanched almonds and glacé cherries for decorating—as required

Method. Put the flour in a bowl. Make a well. Pour in the yeast dissolved in the warm milk. Beat in the eggs,

E

one at a time, with your fingers until the dough is smooth. Cover the bowl with a damp cloth and leave in a warm place to rise for 1 hour, or until the dough has doubled itself.

Knock the dough down and add the sugar and the salt and butter (softened between the fingers but not melted). Beat and slap until the butter is all mixed in smoothly.

Butter a ring mould, or other suitable light cake tin, and dust heavily with the chopped almonds. Pour in the dough. Prove until it has doubled in size and bake for 20 minutes in a very hot oven, covering the cake with butter papers to stop the top from burning.

Meanwhile, make the syrup by gently boiling the water and sugar together (stirring continuously until the sugar is dissolved) for 10 minutes. Then add the rum and allow to cool a little.

As soon as the cake is out of the oven and removed from its mould and set upon its wire tray, spoon the syrup over it. Finally, decorate with the almonds and cherries.

EASTER BREAD (Russia)

To make 1 medium-sized loaf.

Ingredients: 1 oz. yeast
¼ pint warm milk
½ lb. flour (more if required)
3 oz. butter
3 oz. sugar

Coffee Breads from Abroad

3 egg yolks
4 oz. candied peel
Pinch of salt

Method. Dissolve the yeast in the warm milk. Mix in a spoonful or so of the flour. Leave to rise for 30 minutes.

Beat the egg yolks, the salt, the sugar and the butter (warmed and liquid but not too hot) together.

Combine the two mixtures and with the fingers and hand beat in the rest of the flour. You want a soft, smooth dough. Add the peel. Cover with a damp cloth and leave to rise for 1½ hours, or until the dough has doubled itself.

Shape either into a long loaf or into a plait and prove on a lightly floured baking sheet for 30 minutes. Brush with beaten egg and milk and bake for 30 to 40 minutes in a moderate to fairly hot oven.

GUGELHUPF (Austria)

Almost any yeast cake, baked in the typical centre tube mould with the fluted wall, qualifies as a Gugelhupf. But the following is a very pleasant coffee cake, and if you have no proper mould an ordinary, plain, centre tube or ring mould will do very nicely.

To make 1 medium-sized cake.

Ingredients: 1 oz. yeast
⅛ pint warm milk
2 oz. butter or margarine, melted but cool
2 oz. sugar

Coffee Breads from Abroad

2 eggs
8 oz. flour
The zest and juice of 1 orange
2 oz. seedless raisins, soaked in a little water
  or rum
Breadcrumbs and icing sugar

Method. Dissolve the yeast in the warm milk. Mix in a spoonful or so of the flour and allow the mixture to rise for half an hour in a warm place.

Add, beating thoroughly or whisking after each addition, the butter, the eggs, the sugar, the orange juice and zest, and the raisins. And finally beat in the rest of the flour, gradually, slapping it in with the fingers.

This should be a very slack dough, that you can almost pour.

Grease the mould thoroughly and dust it with breadcrumbs.

Fill it half full with the dough. Let it rise for about an hour or until the dough has risen to the top of the mould. Then bake in a moderate oven for 30 to 40 minutes.

Let it cool on a wire rack and dust lightly with icing sugar to decorate.

Coffee Breads from Abroad

<small>STREUSEL CAKE</small> (Austria)

Like the Gugelhupf recipe this is, as it were, a sample one. There must be hundreds of Streusel recipes.

To make 1 medium-sized cake.

Ingredients: 1. The dough.

- 1 oz. yeast
- $\frac{1}{8}$ pint milk
- 2 tablespoons sugar
- Large pinch salt
- 2 eggs, well beaten
- 4 oz. butter or margarine, melted and cooled
- Zest of 1 lemon
- About 8 oz. flour

2. The streusel.

- 1 oz. butter
- 1 oz. flour
- 6 oz. sugar
- 1 tablespoon cinnamon powder
- And you will need melted butter for brushing

Method. Dissolve the yeast in the lukewarm milk. Stir in the sugar and the salt and leave mixture to stand for a few minutes.

Beat in the eggs, the lemon zest and the butter. Gradually knead in the flour. Knead until very soft and smooth and elastic. Cover with a cloth and leave in a warm place to rise for 1½ hours.

Then knock down and roll out on a liberally floured

baking pan—1 Swiss roll tin or two ordinary sponge tins will take this amount of dough nicely.

Prove for 30 minutes.

And while the cake is proving prepare the streusel. Cut the ingredients together until they are crumbly.

Brush the top of the cake with melted butter and sprinkle heavily with the streusel. Bake in a moderate or fairly hot oven for about 30 minutes.

POPPY SEED BREAD (Austria)

To make 1 large loaf or several smaller ones—according to taste.

Ingredients: 1 oz. yeast
¼ pint warm milk
2 oz. sugar
1 teaspoonful salt
1 egg
About ¾ lb. flour
2 oz. butter or margarine, melted and cooled
And 1 egg, beaten with water, for brushing, and a quantity of poppy seeds

Method. Dissolve the yeast in the milk. Stir in the sugar and the salt. Leave to stand for a few minutes in moderate warmth. Add the egg, well beaten, and mix and add the flour and the butter and knead until you have a nice, smooth, creamy dough.

Leave to rise for 30 minutes or so. Then knock down

and knead again for a few minutes. Leave to rise for 1½ hours or until the dough has doubled itself.

Then knock down and divide into three and plait (or make two or three smaller plaits). Prove until doubled in bulk.

Brush with egg and sprinkle heavily with poppy seed. Bake in a moderate oven for about 30 minutes (somewhat less if you have made 2 or 3 loaves).

SAFFRON BREAD (Sweden)

To make 1 large plait or 2 small.

Ingredients: About 8 oz. flour

¼ pint warm milk (scant)

1 oz. fresh yeast

Large pinch of saffron. (Saffron can be bought at most chemists'. It's expensive but a very little goes a very long way)

1 oz. butter or margarine

2 oz. sugar

1 egg

1 dessertspoon ground almonds

1 oz. seedless raisins or 1 oz. candied peel

And, for the topping: 1 egg; a quantity of granulated sugar; and some chopped nuts (almonds for preference)

Method. Dissolve the yeast in half the warm milk and mix in a little of the flour, enough to make a thin paste. Leave to rise in a warm place for 30 minutes.

Coffee Breads from Abroad

Dry the saffron in a cool oven. Pound it with a little sugar. Then stir it in with the rest of the milk, and add it to the yeast mixture.

Whisk the butter, warm and liquid but not too hot, the egg and the rest of the sugar together. Work the butter-egg-sugar into the saffron-yeast mixture. Gradually beat in the flour, kneading briskly until you have a smooth soft dough, all of one good, yellow colour. Knead in the ground almonds and the raisins (plumped in water or rum).

Cover with a cloth and leave to rise in a warm place for $1\frac{1}{2}$ hours, or until the dough has doubled in size.

Knock the dough down and knead for a few minutes. Divide into 3 equal portions (or 6 if you want to make 2 plaits). Roll each out into a long, thin strand and plait.

Prove on a lightly floured baking sheet for about 30 minutes. Brush with beaten egg, sprinkle with chopped nuts and sugar. And bake for 20 to 30 minutes in a fairly hot oven.

STRIEZEL (Austria)

Apparently, there are about as many Striezels as there are provinces in Austria and Bohemia. The following is a recipe for a plain and simple Striezel—you can add nuts, fruit, candied peel, etc., as you fancy. But the important thing is the braiding.

To make one largish Striezel.

Coffee Breads from Abroad

Ingredients: 2 oz. fresh yeast
¼ pint milk
Pinch salt
4 oz. sugar
1 whole egg and 1 egg yolk
4 oz. melted butter or margarine (cool)
1 lb. flour—more as required
1 egg white beaten with a teaspoon of milk

Method. Dissolve the yeast in the milk. Add the sugar and the salt and stir until the sugar is all melted. Leave to stand in a warm place for 10 minutes or so—until the mixture starts to bubble.

Beat in the whole egg and the yolk. Beat in a little of the flour and the butter. Gradually work in the rest of the flour and knead to a stiff, clean dough. Cover with a damp cloth and leave to rise for an hour in a warm place.

Roll the dough out into a sausage. Cut into half. Cut one half into ¾ and ¼, and the other into ⅔ and ⅓; so that you have four pieces of dough ranging nicely in size.

Take the largest piece first. Divide into four and plait and lay it on a lightly floured baking sheet. Plait the next largest in three strands and place it on top of the first. Plait the third largest piece in three strands and put that on top of the second. Lastly, twist the smallest bit in two strands and put that on top of all. Press the whole down a little and shape gently but firmly into an oval.

Coffee Breads from Abroad

Prove for 45 minutes or an hour, until the Striezel is about doubled in size. Brush with the egg white and milk and bake in a very hot oven for 15 minutes and then in a moderate oven for another 30 or 40 minutes.

SWEDISH COFFEE BREAD

To make one Coffee Twist, one Cinnamon Ring and about a dozen Fruit and Nut buns.

Ingredients: 1 lb. flour
⅜ pint lukewarm milk
1 oz. fresh yeast
3 oz. sugar
Pinch of salt
2 oz. butter or margarine, melted and cool
1 egg for brushing
A quantity of chopped nuts, currants, sultanas and cinnamon powder. Sugar. About 1 oz. melted butter or margarine

Method. Put the flour in a bowl. Add the sugar and salt and mix. Make a well. Pour in the yeast, creamed in a little of the milk, and the butter. Mix with a spoon until all the milk and fat have been absorbed. Then cover with a damp cloth and leave to rise in a warm place for 2 hours—or overnight, or until the dough has doubled in size.

Then knead the dough briskly until it is soft and smooth. Divide into 3 portions. You can make something different with each bit.

Coffee Breads from Abroad

Coffee Twist. Take ⅓ dough and divide into 3 equal portions. Roll each piece into a strand. Plait lightly and let the twist prove on a baking sheet for ¾ hour. Brush with beaten egg, sprinkle with sugar and chopped nuts and bake in a moderate oven for 15 to 20 minutes.

Cinnamon Ring. Take ⅓ dough and roll out as thinly as possible on a floured board. Brush with melted butter and sprinkle heavily with sugar and cinnamon. Roll up like a Swiss Roll and join the ends together to make a ring. Brush the ends with beaten egg to make sure they seal. Put the ring on a baking sheet to prove. Decorate by cutting roll with scissors and pulling the leaves thus formed to alternate sides. Prove for ¾ hour. Brush with beaten egg and bake in a moderate oven for 15 to 20 minutes.

Fruit and Nut buns. Take the remaining ⅓ dough and roll out as thinly as possible on the floured board. Brush with melted butter and sprinkle heavily with sugar, currants, sultanas and chopped nuts. Roll up like a Swiss Roll and cut into small buns. Decorate each bun with scissors according to your fancy. Prove on a baking sheet for ¾ hour. Brush with egg and bake in a hot oven for 5 or 10 minutes.

This Swedish Coffee Bread is a wonderful example of the joys of baking with yeast. The making of the dough is simple and troublefree and if you don't want to use it all at one moment, you can leave it. You could start the dough off one evening before going to bed—5 or 10

75

Coffee Breads from Abroad

minutes labour, less perhaps—and the following day, without much additional labour, you could have a fresh-baked Coffee Twist for breakfast, a fresh-baked Cinnamon Ring with your coffee after lunch, and fresh-baked Fruit and Nut buns for tea!

5

A Miscellany

CHALLAH (Jewish Sabbath Bread)

To make one small Challah.

Ingredients: ½ lb. flour
        1 teaspoon salt
        1 teaspoon sugar
        2 oz. vegetable fat melted, and cool
        ⅛ pint warm water (approx.)
        1 oz. yeast

A Miscellany

1 egg
Pinch of saffron
A quantity of Poppy seeds and the yolk of
an egg, beaten

Method. Dry the saffron in a cool oven, pound with the
sugar. Dissolve the yeast in the warm water. Combine
the yeast water and the saffron sugar and stir.

Put the flour in a bowl and make a well. Pour in the
yeast-saffron, the fat and the egg, lightly beaten. Add
the salt and knead to a good, clean, stiff dough. Adding
more water if necessary. Cover with a damp cloth and
leave in a warm place to rise for 1½ hours or until the
dough has doubled itself.

Knock the dough down and divide into 3, 5 or 7 and
plait—the knobblier the loaf is the better.

Let it prove on a lightly floured baking sheet in
moderate warmth for 45 minutes. Brush with egg yolk
and sprinkle heavily with poppy seeds and bake—for
about 15 minutes in a hot oven, and then another 45
minutes in a moderate oven.

COULIBIAC (Russia)

Ingredients: ¼ pint milk
¼ lb. flour
½ oz. yeast
3 eggs
4 oz. butter, margarine or lard, melted and
cooled

½ to ¾ lb. flour
1 dessertspoon salt
1 egg yolk for brushing
And the filling. Meat, fish, mushrooms,
    olives, hard-boiled eggs, etc.

Method. Dissolve the yeast in the milk which should be lukewarm. Add the ¼ lb. flour and beat till smooth. Leave to rise for 30 minutes. Add the eggs, the salt, the fat and the flour as required to make a soft, smooth dough. Knead thoroughly. Cover with a cloth and leave to rise in a warm place for 1½ hours or until the dough has doubled itself.

Prepare the filling.

Roll the dough out in a square on a floured board to a thickness of about ¼ inch. Put the filling in layers in the middle. Wrap the dough up round the filling like wrapping up a parcel (seal the joins with egg or milk). Make two steam vents in the top. Paint with egg yolk and bake (without proving) in a hot oven for 40 to 50 minutes.

CARAWAY SEED BREAD (1) (Sweden)

To make 1 medium-sized loaf.

Ingredients: 2 oz. moist brown sugar
    ¼ pint water
    Dessertspoon caraway seeds
    Zest of 1 orange
    1 oz. butter or margarine

Small pinch salt

1 oz. yeast dissolved in a little warm water

½ to ¾ lb. flour. (Half of which can be rye
flour, if you like)

Method. Boil the sugar, the water, the orange zest, the
butter and the caraway seeds for about 3 minutes. Let
the mixture cool to lukewarm. Add the salt, the dissolved yeast and ¼ lb. of the flour. Beat until smooth.
Cover with a cloth and leave to rise in a warm place
until doubled in size (1½ hours).

Knead in as much of the remaining flour as is required to make a nice, smooth dough. Half fill a large
bread tin with the dough and prove for 45 minutes.
Bake in a moderate oven for 45 minutes or 1 hour.

CARAWAY SEED BREAD (2)

To make 1 medium-sized loaf

Ingredients: ¼ pint lukewarm milk

2 oz. butter or margarine, melted but cool

2 oz. sugar

Teaspoon salt

1 oz. yeast

Tablespoon caraway seeds

½ to ¾ lb. flour

Method. Dissolve the yeast in the milk. Add the sugar,
the salt and a spoonful or two of the flour and beat until
smooth. Leave to rise for 20 minutes or so.

Put most of the flour in a bowl. Mix in the caraway seeds. Make a well. Pour in the yeast mixture and the fat and knead, adding more flour if required, until you have a good, smooth, stiff dough. Cover with a cloth and leave to rise in a warm place for 1½ hours, or until the dough has doubled itself.

Shape into a long roll and prove on a lightly floured baking sheet for 30 to 45 minutes. Bake for 45 to 55 minutes in a moderate oven.

PIZZA (Italy)

To make 1 medium-sized pizza, enough for 4 persons.

Ingredients:

The dough: ½ lb. flour
1 oz. yeast dissolved in a little warm water
Tablespoon olive oil
Heaped teaspoon salt
Warm water as required

The filling: (the following is for Pizza Alla Napolitana, but of course there are many different sorts of Pizza and almost you can use what you fancy)
1 lb. tomatoes
1 clove garlic, chopped
2 oz. grated Parmesan cheese
1 small tin fillets of anchovy
Marjoram

A Miscellany

Salt and pepper
Oil for frying

Method. The dough. Put the flour in a bowl and beat in the salt and the olive oil. Make a well. Pour in the yeast and the olive oil and water as required to make a nice, smooth, softish dough. Cover with a cloth and leave to rise in a warm place for 1½ hours or overnight or until suppertime, etc.

The filling. Remove the skins of the tomatoes and chop. Fry them in a pan with the olive oil and garlic. Add the cheese and the anchovies just before the tomatoes are ready. Add salt and pepper and a sprig of marjoram and simmer for 20 to 30 minutes.

Now roll the dough out on to a well-greased baking tin. Cover with the filling and bake (without proving) for 15 to 20 minutes in a hot oven.

RUM BABA (France)

To make a dozen small babas (Castle pudding tin size) or one largish baba.

Ingredients: 4 oz. flour
1 oz. yeast
⅛ pint milk
2 eggs
2 oz. butter or margarine (softened but not melted)
Pinch of salt
2 oz. sugar
1 oz. candied peel

1 oz. currants and 1 oz. seedless raisins,
plumped in a little rum
For the syrup—4 oz. sugar
3 tablespoons water
1 tablespoon rum

Method. Dissolve the yeast in the warm milk and add to the flour. Beat in the 2 eggs, slapping with the fingers until the whole is smooth and of uniform colour. Cover with a cloth and leave to rise in a warm place for 45 minutes.

Add the sugar, the salt and the softened butter and beat, slapping with fingers, until all is mixed and smooth. Then add the fruit and mix thoroughly.

To make one large baba—pour the mixture into a well-buttered ring mould or other light cake tin. Half fill the mould. Prove until doubled and bake in a hot oven for 45 minutes, covering the top with butter papers to stop it burning if necessary.

To make small babas—half fill well-buttered Castle pudding tins with the mixture. Prove until doubled and bake in a hot oven for about 15 minutes.

Remove the cakes from their tins (if they don't slip out easily wrap them up in cloths for 10 minutes or so) and let them cool on a wire rack.

Make the syrup—boil the water and sugar gently together for 10 minutes, then remove from heat and add the rum, stirring all the time.

Pour the syrup over the large baba. Or dip the small ones into it.

A Miscellany

SALT STICKS (Austria)

To make 3 to 4 dozen.

Ingredients: 1 oz. yeast
$\frac{1}{4}$ pint lukewarm milk
2 oz. butter or margarine, melted but cool
Teaspoon sugar
Teaspoon salt
About $\frac{1}{2}$ lb. flour
Poppy Seeds and Salt

Method. Dissolve the yeast in a little of the milk and leave to stand for a few minutes.

Put the rest of the milk, the butter, the salt and the sugar in a bowl. Make sure it's not too hot. Stir in the yeast and leave to stand until it bubbles.

Beat in the flour gradually—as much as is required. And knead to a soft, smooth dough. Cover with a damp cloth and leave to rise $1\frac{1}{2}$ hours.

Knock the dough together and roll out on a floured board to $\frac{1}{4}$-inch thickness, or thinner. Cut into 4-inch squares. Divide the squares into two triangles. Roll up each triangle as for a croissant, but don't shape into crescents, leave them straight.

Prove on a lightly floured baking sheet for 15 minutes. Brush with water and sprinkle with salt and poppy seeds and bake for 10 to 15 minutes in a hot oven.

Salt Sticks make pleasant supper rolls, and if you make them very small they go down well with sherry or cocktails.

Index

Index